READERS FOR TEENS

Let's Do It Together

Luiz H. Rose

Maiza Fatureto

Tereza Sekiya

Series coordinator
Sérgio Varela

CAMBRIDGE
UNIVERSITY PRESS

University Printing House, Cambridge CB2 8BS, United Kingdom

One Liberty Plaza, 20th Floor, New York, NY 10006, USA

477 Williamstown Road, Port Melbourne, VIC 3207, Australia

314–321, 3rd Floor, Plot 3, Splendor Forum, Jasola District Centre,
New Delhi – 110025, India

79 Anson Road, #06–04/06, Singapore 079906

Cambridge University Press is part of the University of Cambridge.

It furthers the University's mission by disseminating knowledge in the pursuit of
education, learning and research at the highest international levels of excellence.

http://cambridge.org/elt/readersforteens/

© Cambridge University Press 2008

This publication is in copyright. Subject to statutory exception
and to the provisions of relevant collective licensing agreements,
no reproduction of any part may take place without the written
permission of Cambridge University Press.

First published 2008

20 19 18 17 16 15 14 13 12 11 10

Printed in the United Kingdom by Latimer Trend

A catalogue record for this publication is available from the British Library

ISBN 978-0-521-72142-4 paperback

Cambridge University Press has no responsibility for the persistence or accuracy
of URLs for external or third-party internet websites referred to in this publication,
and does not guarantee that any content on such websites is, or will remain,
accurate or appropriate.

Illustrations by Cris Eich

Art direction, book design and layout services: A+ Comunicação, Brazil

Contents

Chapter 1
The blackout — 5

Chapter 2
The box — 8

Chapter 3
An Amazon Indian legend — 11

Chapter 4
A letter to a president — 16

Chapter 5
From darkness to light — 19

Chapter 1
The blackout

The Costas live in an apartment in São Paulo, a large city in Brazil. Mr. Costa is a computer programmer. Mrs. Costa, his wife, writes articles for a newspaper. They have three teenage kids: Marcos (the oldest), Roberto (the middle child), and Maria (the youngest).

One evening, the Costa family was spending a quiet night at home when the power (electricity) went out.

"Mom, what happened to the lights?" asked Maria. "I can't do my homework!"

"I don't know what happened to the power, Maria," said Mrs. Costa. "Almost two hours of hard work and my article is gone. What now? What will we do if the power doesn't come back on soon? What will I say to the newspaper editor? How will you finish your homework?"

asked Mrs. Costa.

"Yeah, why did this have to happen now? I was winning! I had a high score on this video game. I'll never get this score again!" said Roberto.

Marcos came into the living room. "I don't believe it! I was just writing an e-mail to my friend when the power went out," said Marcos. "What happened?"

Mr. Costa was busy doing some paperwork in his office, but he had to stop, too.

A blackout prevented the whole family from doing their evening activities.

Chapter 2
The box

Mr. Costa asked Marcos to get some candles in the kitchen. Mrs. Costa lit the candles and put them on the coffee table. The whole family was upset because of the blackout. They all sat down and looked at each other. They had nothing to do.

"I think there's a blackout in the whole neighborhood. So, let's all do something together. I have an idea. I have something special I can show you," said Mr. Costa. "Wait here."

When Mr. Costa came back into the living room he was carrying an old wooden box. "This box has many special things in it," said Mr. Costa. Everybody was curious.

Mr. Costa slowly opened the box. He took out an old black-and-white photo.

Mr. Costa showed the photo to the rest of his family. It was a picture of a huge tree.

"This photo reminds me of the great moments I had listening to my grandfather's stories when I was a child. At that time we used to do things differently. We didn't watch TV and we didn't have computers.  We used to spend more time with the family," Mr. Costa said. "Let me tell you one of the many interesting stories my grandfather used to tell me."

"Dad, does this story happen in a place where there isn't any power?" Roberto asked.

"Well, Roberto, it does. You see, in the beginning, according to an Amazon Indian legend, there was only darkness," Mr. Costa answered.

The whole family was quiet and curious to know more.

Chapter 3
An Amazon Indian legend

"Once upon a time, there was an enormous tree in the Amazon region. The tree was called the kapok tree. The kapok tree was very tall and had very long branches that blocked the sun's light from reaching the Earth. There was only darkness for people on Earth. Life on Earth was very sad," Mr. Costa said.

"It was just like it is now. There was no light," Maria said.

"That's right, Maria. Right now, we can imagine what it was like for them, can't we?" Mr. Costa said.

Mr. Costa continued the story, "One day, there was a big thunderstorm with lots of thunder and lightning. The Indians were afraid."

"What happened to the kapok tree?" Marcos asked.

"Well, strong lightning hit the kapok tree and it fell down. The Amazon Indian tribes believed that the tree became the Amazon River.  The tree's branches became the smaller rivers in the Amazon region," Mr. Costa said. "And when the tree fell down, there was finally light for the people. Everyone was very happy."

"Is that the end?" asked Roberto.

"Yes, it is," said Mr. Costa. "You liked the story, didn't you?"

"Yeah," the children answered.

"It's a very nice story," said Mrs. Costa. "I was writing an article about some of the problems in the Amazon rainforest when the power went out. Unfortunately, the Amazon region has a lot of problems. For example, people are cutting down too many trees and there are too many fires – the environment is being destroyed."

"That's too bad," Marcos said. "What can we do to help the Amazon?"

"That's a difficult question to answer. To keep what we have, first we have to understand that the Earth is very important," Mrs. Costa replied. "Nature is precious and we need to keep it safe."

"Hmm…that reminds me of another story that my grandfather used to tell me about a Native American tribe in the U.S.," Mr. Costa said.

"Tell us the story, Dad," Roberto said.

Chapter 4
A letter to a president

Mr. Costa began the story, "Over two hundred years ago, the president of the United States, George Washington, said he wanted to buy some land from a Native American Indian tribe in the U.S. The chief of the tribe – Chief Seattle – sent a letter to the president."

"What did the letter say?" asked Marcos.

"In the letter, Chief Seattle told the president that selling or buying the land was a strange idea. His people believed that everything – the land, the animals, the flowers, and the sky – belonged to the Earth. It was not for sale," said Mr. Costa.

"Hmm… I never thought of that," said Maria. "What else did Chief Seattle say?"

"Well, Chief Seattle also told President Washington that what happens to the Earth

happens to everyone," said Mr. Costa. "The Earth doesn't belong to the people; the people belong to the Earth."

"That is very true," said Mrs. Costa.

"Yes, it is," said Mr. Costa. "We all need to remember that the Earth is very important."

"Yes, we do. We need to take special care of it," added Roberto.

Chapter 5
From darkness to light

Suddenly, the power came back on. The Costas sat quietly on the living room floor. They listened to the noises coming from the computer and from the other electronic things in the apartment.

"Mom, can we stay here and listen to another story?" Maria asked.

"You really enjoyed the stories, didn't you?" Mrs. Costa asked.

"I liked spending time with you all. I don't want to play my video game anymore," Roberto commented.

"Unfortunately, I have to finish my work," Mr. Costa said.

"And I have to finish writing my article on problems in the Amazon rainforest," Mrs. Costa added.

"Oh, can we help you finish the article?" Maria asked.

"Sure. That's a great idea," Mrs. Costa answered.

"Maybe you could give some ideas on how to protect the environment in your article," Marcos said.

"That's a good idea," Mrs. Costa said.

"Mom, can I help protect nature, too?" asked Maria.

"Yes, we can all help to protect nature," Mrs. Costa answered. "There are several ways we can help. Can you think of any?" Mrs. Costa asked her children.

"Hmm… recycle paper, cans, and bottles," Marcos said.

"Yes. That's right. And what about the lights and the water?" Mrs. Costa asked.

"We can turn off the lights when we are not in the room," Maria said.

"Excellent, Maria," Mrs. Costa said.

"And be more careful with the water when we take a shower or wash our hands," Roberto added.

"Great, Roberto," Mrs. Costa said.

"Why don't we make a list of more things we can do to help the Earth?" Mrs. Costa suggested.

"OK, I'll go to my room and make a list," Roberto said.

"No, don't leave. Let's do it together!" Marcos said.

Marcos looked at his sister and parents enthusiastically. They all had the same look – there was light in their eyes! Finally, they said, "Yes, let's do it together!"